My Little Golden Book About
# New York City

## By Apple Jordan
## Illustrated by Melanie Demmer

A GOLDEN BOOK · NEW YORK

Text copyright © 2021 by Penguin Random House LLC
Cover and interior illustrations copyright © 2021 by Melanie Demmer
All rights reserved. Published in the United States by Golden Books, an imprint of
Random House Children's Books, a division of Penguin Random House LLC, 1745 Broadway,
New York, NY 10019. Golden Books, A Golden Book, A Little Golden Book, the G colophon,
and the distinctive gold spine are registered trademarks of Penguin Random House LLC.
rhcbooks.com
Educators and librarians, for a variety of teaching tools, visit us at RHTeachersLibrarians.com
Library of Congress Control Number: 2020945409
ISBN 978-0-593-30447-1 (trade) — ISBN 978-0-593-30448-8 (ebook)
Printed in the United States of America
10 9 8 7 6 5 4 3 2

Hi! My name is Poppy the Pigeon, and I live way up here, atop this skyscraper in the middle of New York City. Some call this place the Big Apple. I call it home.

I've flown over every inch of this great city. Come on, I'll show you around.

Our first stop is **Times Square**. This place is full of bright lights, neon signs, and *lots* of people. More than 300,000 of them walk around here each day!

That street running through Times Square is **Broadway**. There are loads of theaters on and around Broadway where you can see some of the best plays and musicals in the world.

Now let's visit my friends Patience and
Fortitude. Those are the two lions guarding
the **New York Public Library**. The city's largest
library was built in 1911—that means my lion
friends are more than 110 years old!

Not far away is the **Empire State Building**. When it was built in 1931, it was the tallest skyscraper in the world. It may not be the tallest building anymore, but you can still get an impressive bird's-eye view of the city from the top. I'll fly up there to meet you—you can take the elevator!

Next stop is **Rockefeller Center**. In the wintertime, people come here from all over the world to get their picture taken in front of the enormous Christmas tree and go ice-skating.

On the other side of the city, we can take a stroll along the **High Line**. This unique park was built on an abandoned train line that runs above the city streets.

Now let's go down *below* the city streets and ride a subway train. We can hop on and head to . . .

. . . **Chinatown**—a neighborhood full of outdoor markets, and restaurants serving up plates of delicious noodles and dim sum. *Yum!*

# Welcome to *Little Italy*

For dessert, let's go to **Little Italy**. Here you'll find bakeries with mouthwatering treats like tiramisu, cannoli, zeppole, and gelato. *Mmm!* This sure beats birdseed!

Need a break from the crowded streets? Let's fly back uptown and spend some time among the trees and green grass in **Central Park**. While we're here, we can visit my penguin friends at the **Central Park Zoo**,

ride on the carousel,

and take a relaxing boat ride across the lake.

Feeling rested? Great! We still have a lot more to see!

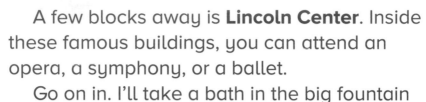

A few blocks away is **Lincoln Center**. Inside these famous buildings, you can attend an opera, a symphony, or a ballet.

Go on in. I'll take a bath in the big fountain outside while I wait for you.

New York City is famous for its live performances *and* for its countless museums. Let me show you two of my favorites.

**The Metropolitan Museum of Art** has more than two million works of art inside, from ancient sculptures to knights in shining armor to modern paintings.

On the other side of town is the **American Museum of Natural History**, where you'll find fossils of my prehistoric ancestors—the dinosaurs!

Next stop uptown is the landmark **Apollo Theater** in **Harlem**. From Ella Fitzgerald to Louis Armstrong to Aretha Franklin, some of the greatest singers and musicians in the world have performed here.

We're not done yet! Let's leave **Manhattan** and explore the outer boroughs.

We can stop and smell the roses at the **New York Botanical Garden** in the **Bronx,**

see the Unisphere from the 1964 World's Fair in **Flushing Meadows Corona Park** in **Queens,**

ride the Cyclone roller coaster
in **Coney Island** in **Brooklyn** . . .

CYCLONE

. . . and take a ferry to **Staten Island** to see one of the best views of the **Statue of Liberty** along the way. This giant statue has stood as a symbol of hope and freedom for all since 1886.

Just north of Lady Liberty in New York Harbor is **Ellis Island**. Here you can tour the **National Museum of Immigration** and see where many of our country's immigrants entered the United States beginning in 1892.

*Phew!* We sure packed a lot into one day. Whether you're a night owl or an early bird, there's always something to see and do in New York City. Thanks for letting me show you around!